D1329902

It's Already There

Where Are You?

It's Already There

Where Are You?

By
Rod Parsley

RESUL/S
P U B L I S H I N G

Columbus, Ohio

It's Already There: Where Are You?
Copyright © 2005 by Rod Parsley
All rights reserved
Printed in the United States of America
ISBN 1-933336-00-5

Published by:
Results Publishing
World Harvest Church
P.O. Box 32932
Columbus, Ohio 43232 USA

This book or parts thereof may not be reproduced in any form without written permission from the publisher.

Unless otherwise indicated, all Scripture references are from the King James Version of the Bible.

TABLE OF CONTENTS

Introduction

YOU MUST START WHAT GOD HAS FINISHED

Andrew was devastated when his wife asked him for a divorce. He'd married Maureen, a single mother of two children, with high hopes for a family of his own. Though the family always struggled financially, he had gladly supported his wife's daughter through numerous medical problems, and he had endured the devastation her son's addictions to alcohol and drugs and had wrought on the family. But that wasn't enough for Maureen. One early November evening she told him, "I want out." By which she meant, she wanted *him* out. She told him he could stay through the spring (so he could help pay the winter heating bills), but after that he would have to move out.

His only family in the area was his younger brother, who lived about forty-five minutes away.

Andrew was reluctant to reach out. He'd kept his extended family distant during his marriage, and he'd had only minimal contact with his young nephew and niece. That didn't change until he received an unusual request from his sister-in-law: come watch the kids on a Friday night so Andrew's brother and his wife could attend a party with friends.

"I can't explain why I drew closer to God during that period," Andrew said, "but I did. Even though I was grieving the loss of my marriage, and facing the prospect of even greater financial struggles, I was spending more time in the Word and in prayer than I had in several years. When my brother asked me to watch his kids, I didn't know what to think. I had never watched anyone else's kids before. But it was immediately clear to me that my response was a matter of obedience to God. I was scared, but I said yes."

Andrew and his niece and nephew ordered pizza and watched movies until bedtime. Late in the evening Andrew's 5-year-old niece, whom he'd barely interacted with throughout his marriage, walked over to the couch, kissed him on the cheek and said, "I love you, Uncle Andrew." And with that kiss, God had rewarded Andrew's obedience — not with the begrudging acceptance of his brother's family, but with heartfelt, unconditional love.

Andrew spent more time at his brother's house in the next few months than he had in the several years prior. He frequently took his niece and nephew to indoor playlands and to movies. Those times helped him heal from the toll his marriage had taken on him, and gave him hope that he was still capable of loving and being loved.

Today, Andrew says his niece's kiss was the moment he knew God would sustain him through the dark days ahead. And they *were* dark. But God showed Andrew that as long as he obeyed Him, He would deliver Andrew from the devastation he was experiencing and bring him continued rewards for his obedience to Him. And He has!

Today, Andrew is remarried and has a bustling young family of his own. Emotionally and financially, his marriage to Maureen virtually bankrupted him. But as a result of his obedience, God has richly prospered Andrew in both areas. As Andrew has been faithful to God's calling on his life, He has provided him with a beautiful home and the means to give generously to God's work. Now he ministers to others as part of the staff here at World Harvest Church. He's just one example of the principles I want to share with you in this book.

I believe many Christians fail to understand the biblical principles of obedience. I believe if we truly grasped what the Word of God has to say about His provision and our obedience, we would begin to walk out of the land of lack and into the reality of God's supernatural blessing!

In the Gospel of Mark, Jesus shared a powerful parable:

> *And he said, So is the kingdom of God, as if a man should cast seed into the ground; And should sleep, and rise night and day, and the seed should spring and grow up, he knoweth not how. For the earth bringeth forth fruit of herself; first the blade, then the ear, after that the full corn in the ear. But when the fruit is brought forth, immediately he putteth in the sickle, because the harvest is come.*
> —*Mark 4:26-29*

There is a harvest waiting for you. In the heavenly pavilions of glory, His hand opened wide, the Lord has something for you. He's not going to create something for you when you decide to obey him. It's *already there.* He's simply waiting for your act of obedience—your casting of a seed—to give it to you.

The apostle Peter told the early church, and he tells us,

> *To whom coming, as unto a living stone, disallowed indeed of men, but chosen of God, and precious, Ye also, as lively stones, are built up a spiritual house, an holy priesthood, to offer up spiritual sacrifices, acceptable to God by Jesus Christ. Wherefore also it is contained in the scripture, Behold, I lay in Sion a chief corner stone, elect, precious: and he that believeth on him shall not be confounded. Unto you therefore which believe he is precious: but unto them which be disobedient, the stone which the builders disallowed, the same is made the head of the corner,*

11

And a stone of stumbling, and a rock of offence, even to them which stumble at the word, being disobedient: whereunto also they were appointed. But ye are a chosen generation, a royal priesthood, an holy nation, a peculiar people; that ye should shew forth the praises of him who hath called you out of darkness into his marvellous light: Which in time past were not a people, but are now the people of God: which had not obtained mercy, but now have obtained mercy.

—1 Peter 2:4-10

We "peculiar people" have all of the rights and privileges of the covenant to receive the rewards of our obedience! You and I are part of the final generation destined to experience to the manifestation of Almighty God. We've been called to the kingdom for such a time as this!

My friend, your breakthrough is one of the last bastions of the enemy's resistance before Christ's imminent return. Your adversary wants you to believe rewards in this life here on earth aren't part of Christianity. But it's not true! We are His heirs, and God longs to open His great storehouse of wealth to us. He waits only for us to plant a seed— to obey Him. He's already arranged for us to receive His abundant blessing. *It's already there.* We only need, through obedience, to start the work that our Heavenly Father has already finished.

As you read this book, I pray that you will discover just how much our heavenly Father wants us to prosper. Through the prophet Isaiah, He said,

> *I will go before thee, and make the crooked places straight: I will break in pieces the gates of brass, and cut in sunder the bars of iron: And I will give thee the treasures of darkness, and hidden riches of secret places, that thou mayest know that I, the Lord, which call thee by thy name, am the God of Israel.*
>
> *—Isaiah 45:2,3*

God wants His people to prosper. He wants *you* to prosper.

These are our final days, and the best is yet to come. A great transfer of wealth about to take place. The Lord wants to reveal to you that your harvest is ready—ready for you to plant a seed.

There's a harvest of salvation, healing, deliverance and financial blessing waiting for you on the other side of the Jordan River. God has given you the anointing and the ability to reap.

It is time to claim what rightfully belongs to you. It's time for you to discover that the provision for your needs is already there.

Chapter One

IT STARTS WITH A SEED

Today, I am privileged to lead seven major ministries, some of which are national and international in scope. But it wasn't always that way. In 1985, I led a church with a few hundred members. Early in that year, I was seeking the Lord regarding our upcoming Easter service and the message He wanted me to bring to the congregation. And, of course, He spoke.

God said to me, "On Easter, you commemorate when I gave my best on Calvary. Declare to the people: on this one day a year, commemorate Me giving My best by giving your best to Me."

These words rang clearly in my spirit. The following Sunday, I shared them with our congregation. Instead of giving our tithe, as we normally did each week, this one time we would give everything to the work of the Lord—100 percent, not just 10 percent. And, I added, I believed God would give us $100,000 in this particular Easter Sunday offering.

When I shared this revelation with our congregation, it seemed like a tremendous step of faith. I felt like I'd really stepped out on a limb—and that the limb could break at any moment. But deep within my spirit, I knew the voice of God. I knew what He'd said to me.

For the next several weeks, in preparation for the confirmation of His Word, I taught on the laws of sowing and reaping. People in the church grasped hold of this truth. Some began to take second jobs. Others fasted and set aside the money they would have spent on food, entertainment, or other luxuries toward that one offering. Still others began to allocate an additional portion of their paycheck each week so that they could give all during this one offering.

Needless to say, word of this incredible move of God traveled fast. When Easter Sunday came, the local news media and skeptics gathered to see what God was *not* going to do! As the offering buckets were passed, my mind raced but my spirit stood strong as I was reminded of the words in

Mark's Gospel:

> *And they went forth, and preached every where, the Lord working with them, and confirming the word with signs following. Amen.*
>
> —*Mark 16:20*

The service continued and it seemed an eternity that I preached and waited for the offering report. Toward the end of the service, having heard no report about the offering, I sent an usher to find out what was taking so long.

He came back a few minutes later and shook his head in disappointment. It felt like my heart sank to my feet. Surely, God did not fail! I looked back at him and muttered, "What do you mean by shaking your head no?" He responded that he couldn't find out anything because the doors to the office were locked!

About that time a dear lady in our church, Mary—who is still a faithful member and worker—came through the door next to the pulpit waving a small piece of paper. As she handed the paper to me, I looked at it, folded it again and laid it aside.

With all eyes watching and everyone waiting, I made the announcement. God had not given us $100,00. Instead, He gave us $140,000!

The God I serve is not a God of just enough. He is the God of more than enough! The scornful and doubting were silenced as the report came. What more could be said? God had proven Himself once again, and we had a supernatural break-through harvest!

From that year forward, the report has been the same, and each time the Lord has abundantly and overwhelmingly provided during our miracle Resurrection Seed offering. And He will do the same for you!

SET-APART SEED

God has sanctified, or set apart, things in His kingdom for use as He sees fit. Our tithe and offerings are no different.

Belshazzar, the Babylonian king, had no regard for what the Lord had sanctified to Himself when he took the golden goblets out of the Lord's temple for his own use. And God pronounced His judgment upon him when He said, *"Thou art weighed in the balances, and art found wanting"* (Daniel 5:27).

Three things happened to Belshazzar as a result of his disobedience. First, the rivers dried up. The rivers represent the power of the Holy Spirit. When we're disobedient to the word of the Lord in our giving or in any other area of our life, it's as though we construct a dam that prevents the blessings of God from flowing freely to us.

Second, Belshazzar's enemies invaded the land through a breach in the wall. Giving is not a take-it-or-leave-it proposition.

Last, Belshazzar died. God cannot bless us beyond our last act of disobedience.

When you put your hand on that which belongs to God, you're going to live a life of want.

God has earmarked your resurrection seed for a specific purpose as well. It has miracle-working power to produce a harvest in your life, because the hand of God has sanctified it. Your seed is anointed and it will return an abundant supply in your life!

RESURRECTION POWER

Throughout the Bible, God has displayed His resurrection power in the lives of His saints and of His own son.

Elisha's dead bones, though bleached and dried by the hot desert sun, had enough resurrection power in them to raise a man from the dead:

> *And Elisha died, and they buried him. And the bands of the Moabites invaded the land at the coming in of the year. And it came to pass, as they were burying a man, that, behold, they spied a band of men; and they cast the man into the sepulchre of Elisha: and when the man was let down, and touched the bones of Elisha, he revived, and stood up on his feet.*
> —*2 Kings 13:20,21*

Lazarus, the friend of Jesus, lay four days wrapped in grave clothes before Jesus raised him from the dead. The Gospel of John declares:

Then when Mary was come where Jesus was, and saw him, she fell down at his feet, saying unto him, Lord, if thou hadst been here, my brother had not died. When Jesus therefore saw her weeping, and the Jews also weeping which came with her, he groaned in the spirit, and was troubled, And said, Where have ye laid him? They said unto him, Lord, come and see. Jesus wept. Then said the Jews, Behold how he loved him! And some of them said, Could not this man, which opened the eyes of the blind, have caused that even this man should not have died? Jesus therefore again groaning in himself cometh to the grave. It was a cave, and a stone lay upon it. Jesus said, Take ye away the stone. Martha, the sister of him that was dead, saith unto him, Lord, by this time he stinketh: for he hath been dead four days. Jesus saith unto her, Said I not unto thee, that, if thou wouldest believe, thou shouldest see the glory of God? Then they took away the stone from the place where the dead was laid. And Jesus lifted up his eyes, and said, Father, I thank thee that thou hast heard me. And I knew that thou hearest me always: but because of the people which stand by I said it, that they may believe that thou hast sent me. And when he thus had spoken, he cried with a loud voice, Lazarus, come forth. And he that was dead came forth, bound hand and foot with graveclothes: and his face was bound about with a napkin. Jesus saith unto them, Loose him, and let him go.

—John 11:32-44

Jesus became a seed as well. In the middle of paradise, Adam chose the archenemy of God in the greatest rebellion ever known to the human family. God came down. In the middle of all of this retrieval, man had wound his moral clock backwards. The image of God had been dashed to pieces. Death came and turned blue the children of men. The locust with its king came to turn blossom into dust.

Man was driven with a flaming sword to the Eastern plains of sterile Eden. He stood in jeopardy before God and all of His Holy angels, and death was the mark upon him. The only hope he had sat before him was the pit from whence he had been dug. But then God gave a propitiation—to Adam, and to us: *"And I will put enmity between thee and the woman, and between thy seed and her seed; it shall bruise thy head, and thou shalt bruise his heel" (Genesis 3:15).*

God promised a sacrifice with hope. It wasn't just some foliage sacrifice. It wasn't payment for just any iniquity. It was something that would take place years and years into the future. It was something of which God said, "It has so much power you can hope on it. You can depend on it. It's going to happen one of these days."

It came in the form of Jesus. When He spoke, death was silenced. It happened in Jairus' bedroom. It happened among the funeral bearers in Nain's streets, and it happened in the burial place in Bethany.

Jairus' daughter, the son of Nain's widow, and Lazarus all rose from the dead. All were just testimonies of what was going to happen down the road.

Our King of kings and Lord of lords became the ultimate resurrection seed. John 12:24 declares,

> *Verily, verily, I say unto you, Except a corn of wheat fall into the ground and die, it abideth alone: but if it die, it bringeth forth much fruit.*

A LITTLE GOES A LONG WAY

Several years ago seeds were found in the tomb of an Egyptian king. They had rested in that tomb for thousands of years, lifeless, without producing any type of harvest.

Scientists decided to try to grow plants from these seeds. They put the seeds in soil, watered them and allowed them to drink in the warm rays of the sun. Within days, the seeds began to sprout leaves and grow into a harvest-producing crop— just as if they'd come from the hardware store instead of an Egyptian tomb!

The result of sowing a resurrection seed is the same in the life of every believer! When the seed leaves your hand, it seems dried, dead, and possibly of little value. But it will never leave your life, because God will multiply it, just as He said He would!

Moses's rod didn't look like much. But God commanded him to stretch it forth and watch the waters of the Red Sea part.

David's slingshot didn't look like much. But it was anointed to slay the Philistine giant.

The little boy's lunch of five loaves and two fishes didn't seem like a lot. But it fed 5,000 and produced leftovers!

And Jesus said unto them, Because of your unbelief: for verily I say unto you, If ye have faith as a grain of mustard seed, ye shall say unto this mountain, Remove hence to yonder place; and it shall remove; and nothing shall be impossible unto you.
—Matthew 17:20

The devil may tell you your seed is of little importance in the economy of God. He may say that the seed in your hand is insignificant and of little worth. That's what he wants you to believe. But if you allow God to touch your seed and sanctify it, He will multiply it and turn it into an abundant breakthrough harvest!

I believe God's people are moving with a new mission. We're about to cross the Jordan and take back everything the devil has stolen from us!

Chapter Two

ARE YOU THERE YET?

God has prepared something for us to move toward. Anytime God requires *anything* of you—in advancement, of extension, or of release—there is something He has already prepared to reward you for that release.

The apostle Paul said Jesus is known as the seed. John notes in his gospel that before the seed entered into its place, the garden was already prepared: *"Now in the place where he was crucified there was a garden; and in the garden a new sepulchre, wherein was never man yet laid" (John 19:41).*

The garden was there. The place of harvesting, the place of blessing, the place of increase was already there prior to the seed being there.

I want to take you on a journey. You may have been on a trip like this many times in your life already. Remember when your family threw its suitcases in the trunk of the car and you piled in and took off for a vacation or a visit to relatives? It really doesn't matter whether the trip was one hour, two hours, five hours, or ten hours. After thirty minutes or so, you or one of your brothers or sisters would ask the driver, *"Are we there yet?"*

That question still rings in the minds of many. They ask, "When am I going to get to the place that God has destined for me to get my increase? When am I going to get my healing? When am I going to get my next level? When am I going to get my answer from God? *When am I going to get there?"*

I want you to know that there is a place called "there." God is a God of divine timing. Wherever He points, He always provides.

In the Old Testament, God specifically encourages and points Elijah to go to an exact location:

> *And Elijah the Tishbite, who was of the inhabitants of Gilead, said unto Ahab, As the Lord God of Israel liveth, before whom I stand, there shall not be dew nor rain these years, but according to my word. And*

the word of the Lord came unto him, saying, Get thee hence, and turn thee eastward, and hide thyself by the brook Cherith, that is before Jordan. And it shall be, that thou shalt drink of the brook; and I have commanded the ravens to feed thee there. So he went and did according unto the word of the Lord: for he went and dwelt by the brook Cherith, that is before Jordan. And the ravens brought him bread and flesh in the morning, and bread and flesh in the evening; and he drank of the brook. And it came to pass after a while, that the brook dried up, because there had been no rain in the land.

And the word of the Lord came unto him, saying, Arise, get thee to Zarephath, which belongeth to Zidon, and dwell there: behold, I have commanded a widow woman there to sustain thee. So he arose and went to Zarephath. And when he came to the gate of the city, behold, the widow

woman was there gathering of sticks: and
he called to her, and said, Fetch me, I pray
thee, a little water in a vessel, that I may
drink.

— *1 Kings 17:1-10*

Notice that God tells Elijah, "I want you to know that you've got to get to a place that I will give you directions to, and when you get there, there will be two things you need for provision. One is water, and one is meat. It is a form of the Spirit and the Word."

But watch what God says. Before you get to that place, He has already provided the nourishment and everything you need when you get there.

God is not just walking with you. God is sitting at the end of your faith, because He's the author and the finisher of our faith. Elijah sits there at the brook until his courage and strength are built up.

God only gives you increase so you can be strong enough to release somebody else out of their situation and their circumstance.

The Spirit of the Lord says,

> *But thou shalt remember the Lord thy God: for it is he that giveth thee power to get wealth, that he may establish his covenant which he sware unto thy fathers, as it is this day.*
>
> *—Deuteronomy 8:18*

I believe you need to say this in your spirit: It's already there. The question is not, "Is God's provision there?" It is. The question is, "Are *you* there, yet?" Because His provision *already there*.

The Bible says that when Elijah got to Zarephath, the widow woman was picking up sticks. She was preparing for a miracle. She may not have realized that God was about to use her to sustain the man of God and change her future forever. Your promise is always waiting *right there*.

In the gospel of Matthew, you'll find a story you've probably heard before, about a woman with an issue of blood:

> *And, behold, a woman, which was diseased with an issue of blood twelve years,*

came behind him, and touched the hem of his garment: For she said within herself, If I may but touch his garment, I shall be whole. But Jesus turned him about, and when he saw her, he said, Daughter, be of good comfort; thy faith hath made thee whole. And the woman was made whole from that hour.

—Matthew 9:20-22

The woman had a disease, but Matthew—and Mark and Luke, for that matter—identify it as an *issue*. I believe that the reason they identified it as an issue is because they wanted it to be relative 2,000 years later. God wanted us to understand that God can deal with our *issues*. But if we don't realize that there is a specific place for that issue to be dealt with, we'll miss something supernatural in our lives.

The Bible says that this woman had an issue for twelve years, but said within herself, "If I can just touch the hem of His garment, I know I'll be made whole." This woman's faith was connected to a specific "there." She said, "If I can get to the hem of His garment, I know that *right there*, everything I need is waiting on me." So the Bible says that she came empty, broken, and desperate. But she also came with faith. If you come to God with faith, He will meet you at the point of your need.

The woman pushed through the crowd. Sometimes we have to press past other people's issues so that we can get to our need and get our need met. She probably had to pass the first issue of doubt—the people in the street who said, "You tried this before." She probably had to pass the second issue of people that knew her, saying, "There she is, trying to make herself well, bless her heart." But she knew if she could get there, that what she needed would be right there.

So she pressed through the crowd, and the Bible says she grabbed the hem of His garment.

Let me tell you something about people. There are four types of people in the world:

- Those who *bide* time.
- Those who *waste* time.
- Those who go back and try to *redeem* time.
- Those who are going to *transcend* time.

There are going to be people who decide, "I'm going to get what I need, and I'm going to get it *right now*. I'm not waiting another day." The woman with the issue of blood was just this type of a woman. She had a spirit of expectation. And the breeding ground for miracles is a spirit of expectation.

She pressed through the crowd and grabbed the hem of His garment. The Greek word we translate "hem" is *kraspedon*. More specifically, it means "a margin." It means a fringe or a tassel, a border. God always brings you to the border. He'll always bring you to the edge. He'll always make you step to where you think you're going to fall off. He always brings you to a place where the enemy says, "This is as far as you can go." But I believe faith can bring us *beyond borders*.

She grabbed hold to the border. She grabbed hold to the *kraspedon*, and she grabbed hold to the place called the finished part.

Now you may ask, "What does that mean, Pastor?" It means this: when the woman touched Jesus's hem, she literally found herself in a different place. She was there where her faith told her she needed to be to get her needs met.

To this point, the only healing that had ever taken place in the Word of God came from Christ extending Himself. Either He reached and touched or He spit and put the mud in someone's eyes. But in this case healing came when a woman, by faith, reached her destination—her *there*.

You have a destination. In the natural realm you have to locate your destination before you can get a ticket and a seat on a plane. And in the spiritual realm, you need to find out where your "there" is. Put your faith out, and when you get there, God will meet you!

Your miracle is waiting on your next extension of faith, because it's *already there*. God's provision is waiting on your obedience.

IT'S ALREADY THERE

Chapter Three

THE HARVEST GENERATION

Several years ago I traveled to Florida to fish with a close friend of mine in the Gulf of Mexico. I could hardly wait to go. I'd preached several nights on the road, away from my family and my church, and I was looking forward to a much-needed rest.

We cast our lines early in the morning. I was so excited I couldn't wait for the first bite. Hours later—red as a lobster and with no fish in sight—I was ready to call it quits. But my friend wasn't. He pulled the throttle on the boat and began racing across the water.

Startled and almost knocked off my feet, I asked him what he was doing and where he was going. He said, "See that pile of wood floating over there? That's where I'm headed."

I thought the sun had gotten the best of my friend. "We haven't caught anything yet," I protested, "and those old boards don't look good enough to eat!"

He responded, "There are fish under those planks."

We stopped and cast our lines into the water. It seemed like just a few seconds passed before the fish began to bite. As quickly as we could reel them in, we caught fish. Once, a big fish jumped out of the water and snatched another fish right off my line!

Amos 9:13 states,

> *Behold, the days come, saith the Lord,*
> *that the plowman shall overtake the reaper,*
> *and the treader of grapes him that soweth*
> *seed; and the mountains shall drop sweet*
> *wine, and all the hills shall melt.*

In these last days, I believe that's what it's going to be like in the body of Christ, and for you personally. You're going to receive your three-fold harvest all at once—so drastically and unexpectedly that you won't even be able to keep up with how God is going to bless you!

It is harvest time not only for souls, but also for everything else in your life. This is the season of harvest. When the grain fields turn golden brown, the harvest cannot sit in the fields for long before being reaped.

The closer we get to the soon and imminent return of Jesus Christ of Nazareth the shorter time will become. Time is going to shrink.

Take, for instance, when someone breaks an arm or a leg. When I broke my arm as a boy, it took nearly eight weeks for it to mend. When it did mend, though, and the doctor took the cast off, atrophy had set in. My newly healed arm was smaller than my other arm, because it had been in the same position all that time. The muscle had begun to waste away.

When this end-time harvest comes, there will be no space of time between when your seed is sown and when you reap your harvest. Just as when my broken arm was restored, your harvest will be restored to new as instantly as the anointing of God can penetrate it!

Just as the treader of grapes tramples grapes under his feet when he hasn't sown any seed yet, as quickly as your seed hits the ground, you're going to harvest it.

God said He would do a quick work in these last days. The harvest is coming quickly. You don't have time to play around in the playpen of mediocrity.

We've had a lot of teaching on sowing, but how much ministry have you heard on reaping? We need to start expecting a return. We need to begin to understand God's Word concerning harvesting, because we are the harvest generation.

TODAY IS THE DAY

On May 15, 1948, the gavel came down in the halls of the United Nations, and Israel once again became a nation. It was the year of Jubilee.

In the Old Testament, in the year of Jubilee, every slave was set free. Every debt was canceled. But most importantly, everything went back to God—their house, their land, their cattle, their sheep, their mind—everything!

When Jesus walked the earth under the anointing of the Holy Spirit, He walked into the synagogue in Nazareth and there He was handed the book of the prophet Isaiah and began to read:

> *And he came to Nazareth, where he had been brought up: and, as his custom was, he went into the synagogue on the sabbath day, and stood up for to read. And there was delivered unto him the book of the prophet Esaias. And when he had opened the book, he found the place where it was written, The Spirit of the Lord is upon me, because he hath anointed me to preach the gospel to the poor; he hath sent me to heal the brokenhearted, to preach deliverance to the captives, and recovering of sight to the blind, to set at liberty them that are bruised, To preach the acceptable year of the Lord.*
>
> *—Luke 4:16-19*

In essence, I believe God was saying, "You've prayed long enough. You've fasted long enough.

Now I'm about to take control of your situation. I'm about to destroy every oppressor. I'm about to loose every bondage in your life."

It was at that point that Jesus closed the book. Why? Because He had just given a revelation of who He was. He went over to the chair reserved for the High Priest and sat down in it. Then He announced, *"This day is this scripture fulfilled in your ears" (Luke 4:21).*

It's time to stop looking at a calendar. When is Jubilee? It is the day you receive a revelation of who Jesus is.

MAKE PREPARATION!

During the Gulf War, the Allied Forces used stealth bombers which were undetectable to enemy radar. One of them was equipped with a laser. That laser would lock in on a target and shoot a beam of light toward it. The light would dissipate and leave behind only minute particles of light undetectable to anything but a smart bomb. The smart bomb would then follow that trace of light and hit its target with pinpoint accuracy. That target had been painted.

In the same way, God said, "I'm going to draw a target on your life. I'm going to paint you so, when you're in the darkness of your midnight hour, my blessing can find you."

God's blessings are about to overtake you with a sudden and unparalleled harvest. You are part of a generation of reapers and the harvest is ready now! We're going to reap what John Wesley, Martin Luther, Howard Carter and Dr. Lester Sumrall sowed.

Get in the fields! The harvest is already there!

You may ask, "How do I reap my harvest?" Here is how:

- **First**, you send forth your angels. They're just waiting to be released by the words of your mouth to go and get what you need. There are things that you have sown for over the years that you are yet to reap.
- **Second**, you need to prophesy in your harvest. Revelation 19:10 says, *"For the testimony of Jesus is the spirit of prophecy."* It was the words that were spoken about Jesus

that brought Him out of that tomb.

God does not intend for His church to have a begging mentality, a missionary-barrel mentality, or a barely-   getting-by mentality. He doesn't want us to walk around wishing we could find the ends, much less make them meet.

There is a revelation that has come to the body of Christ which is leading us from the back of the bus and moving us into the forefront, where we are going to take control. It is the revelation that there is a three-fold harvest —a spiritual harvest, a physical harvest, and a financial harvest—for all who will learn to operate in the truths of faith.

Third John 2 says, *"Beloved, I wish above all things that thou mayest prosper and be in health, even as thy soul prospereth."*

How long will we continue to believe Scriptures like these are for someone else? How long will we continue to rejoice at someone else's miracle? How long until we turn our hands heavenward and begin to take God at His Word and, in faith believing, receive it as our own?

BELIEVE THE WORD

One day, a fellow was in the park reading his Bible when an atheist passed by and asked him, "Why are you reading that book? It's full of contradictions." The believer calmly slid the Bible across the picnic table toward the atheist and said, "Is that right? Open it up and show me one."

The Bible is the infallible, inerrant Word of the living God. The Bible is tried and tested, and though heaven and earth rock and reel like a drunken man, under the pressure of the hour, the Word of God will remain forever!

In order to stand in the midnight of your situation, you must have faith in the unchanging Word of God.

Psalm 89:16 says, *"In thy name shall they rejoice all the day: and in thy righteousness shall they be exalted."*

Isaiah 55:10,11 proclaims,

For as the rain cometh down, and the snow from heaven, and returneth not thith-

er, but watereth the earth, and maketh it bring forth and bud, that it may give seed to the sower, and bread to the eater: So shall my word be that goeth forth out of my mouth: it shall not return unto me void, but it shall accomplish that which I please, and it shall prosper in the thing whereto I sent it.

Great men and women of the faith have clung to the Word of God in their dying hour as their source of hope and comfort. In the midnight hour of the aching, desperate soul, it has been like a well springing up to life, and the miracle harvest they sought for days, months, and maybe even years came from heaven and invaded their life.

It was midnight when Samson possessed the gates of the city. It was midnight when, from the jail cell, it rang as Paul and Silas sang. It was midnight when Boaz was revealed to Ruth as her kinsman redeemer.

Midnight is the perfect time to release a shout of praise. Anyone can sing a tune on a clear day at noon. But I want a song to sing at midnight when trouble is closing in all around.

Perfect faith begins where the will of God is known. Therefore, first and foremost, you must know the will of God through His Word before you can stand in faith toward God.

FAITH'S FOUNDATION STONE

Faith is not some ethereal, philosophical idea floating around out there with Eastern mysticism. It's not complicated at all. You must begin with the building block and foundational stone of, "I know this is God's will."

Hebrews 11:1 says, *"Now, faith is the substance of things hoped for and the evidence of things not seen."* Faith is the favorable and confident expectation of things not perceived with the sensory mechanisms. Why? Because the things you can feel, smell, taste, hear, and see are subject to change. Faith is not subject to change.

Jesus demonstrated this when He healed a leper:

And it came to pass, when he was in a

certain city, behold a man full of leprosy: who seeing Jesus fell on his face, and besought him, saying, Lord, if thou wilt, thou canst make me clean. And he put forth his hand, and touched him, saying, I will: be thou clean. And immediately the leprosy departed from him.

—Luke 5:12,13

This is the only place in the New Testament where Jesus was asked the question, "If you will." In response, Jesus put forth His hand and touched the leper saying, "I will." You'll never find a place in the New Testament where Jesus said, "No, I won't!"

This is the riveting question in the mind of every believer who tries to step from the natural into the supernatural—to walk by faith, not by sight. Most Christians do not struggle with God's ability. Rather they struggle with the questions, "Is it His will to move in my life?" So understanding the will of God will give you the foundational stone upon which you can stand in faith.

The apostle Paul wrote,

For I am not ashamed of the gospel of Christ: for it is the power of God unto salvation to every one that believeth; to the Jew first, and also to the Greek. For therein is the righteousness of God revealed from faith to faith: as it is written, The just shall live by faith.

—*Romans 1:16,17*

The gospel was foundational—it was the basis of Paul's ministry to the Jews as well as the Gentiles.

The Apostle Peter is another wonderful example of this truth:

And when he had sent the multitudes away, he went up into a mountain apart to pray: and when the evening was come, he was there alone. But the ship was now in the midst of the sea, tossed with waves: for the wind was contrary. And in the fourth watch of the night Jesus went unto them, walking on the sea. And when the disciples saw him walking on the sea, they were troubled, saying, It is a spirit; and they cried out for fear. But straightway Jesus spake unto them, saying, Be of good cheer; it is I; be not afraid. And Peter answered him and said, Lord, if it be thou, bid me come unto thee on the water. And he said, Come. And when Peter was come down out of the ship, he walked on the water, to go to Jesus.

—Matthew 14:23-29

Every time you decide to stand upon the Word of God you begin to get a vision of something painted on the inside of you that makes no sense in the natural realm. No one seems to understand you. At times you may not even understand yourself. Like Peter, everyone is telling you that you can't get out of the boat and walk on water.

However, I believe if you were to ask Peter about what just happened he would turn around and tell you, "I didn't walk on the water. Jesus said to me, 'Come.' When He said that, His Word, like an invisible plank, was laid across the top of the water. I didn't walk on the water, I walked upon His Word!"

Walking *on the water* is impossible, but walking *on the Word* is absolutely possible. *"And Jesus looking upon them saith, With men it is impossible, but not with God: for with God all things are possible" (Mark 10:27).*

A couple in our church latched on to the Word of the Lord in faith when they were handed a baby that had a brain stem, but no brain. His head was swollen out as big as his shoulders.

When the doctors handed them their baby, he was given no hope of living—much less any semblance of a normal life. But they had faith in the Word of God, and His ability to give them their harvest.

They believed it wasn't any harder for God to create a brain outside the womb than it is for God to create a brain inside the womb. Today, their son has a fully developed brain. They received their three-fold miracle harvest.

Your Harvest Is "Yes" and "Amen"

Each of us in the body of Christ needs to understand that whenever we ask God anything, His promises are "yes" and "amen" to all who believe. If you can claim one of God's promises, hold on to it with pit-bull faith. Then you can stare the devil down and say, "You can't make me nervous. I know it's God's will. You can't tempt me and say God would never want that. I know it's God's will!"

Will you heal me? Jesus answers, "I will." Will you bless me? Again He declares, "I will." Will you save my children? Jesus hails a resounding, "Yes!"

An Immediate Harvest

How long did it take Jesus to heal the man with leprosy? The Bible says, *"And he put forth his hand, and touched him, saying, I will: be thou clean. And immediately the leprosy departed from him"* *(Luke 5:13).*

God is sending an *immediate* harvest to His people in these last days. Just as Jesus healed the leper, whomever His Spirit touches will receive their three-fold harvest.

Your ability to reap your harvest is not about you. It's about God backing up His Word.

> *God is not a man, that he should lie; neither the son of man, that he should repent: hath he said, and shall he not do it? or hath he spoken, and shall he not make it good?*
>
> *—Numbers 23:19*

God will make good on His promises. He will pour out His abundant harvest in every area of your life!

FAITH TO FRAME YOUR WORLD

By faith, we understand that the worlds were framed. You can frame your world by faith.

We're taking back our spiritual, physical, and

financial harvest that belong to us. How can we do that? Because God doesn't change, and what He promised in His Word He will do!

What do we mean when we say God doesn't change? It means what He was, He is, and what He is, He will be. And, because He never changes, you and I can have faith in His faithfulness.

Moses had great faith in God's faithfulness. Why? He had met God in the desert through a burning bush. He had an experience with Yahweh. Because of that, Moses could respond when God said, "Go tell Pharaoh that I AM sent me."

God never demands faith beyond your experience with Him. He lays your life out with a series of instances where you must apply faith to make it through. Then He proves Himself faithful in that area, so that He can take you to another level.

If you and I are going to have faith, we need to have a revelation of Jesus—we need to know who is talking to us. After we know this, we must know what He said. After we know what He said, then we must know, does He have a track record? Are they faithful to what they have said?

However, once you get to know Jesus and

understand who He is, then you begin to have faith in His Word. After you have walked with Him, you will discover He is Jehovah Raphe, the God that heals you.

Then when the doctor looks at you and tells you, you have cancer and will die, and you can say, "Wait a minute. I have a higher authority. I hear your word, doctor, but there's another word drowning you out. I'm sorry. The frequency's breaking up! I can't hear you. I've got another message coming in, and it declares, 'With His stripes, I am healed.'" Then you can stand on that word when there isn't anything else to stand on. You can hope against hope, and you can believe beyond faith. You can stand steadfast and say, "God declared it. He will establish it, and though heaven and earth shall pass away, His Word shall remain."

When you stand on the word of God, people may laugh at you. When a second opinion is worse than the first, continue to cling to that Word. Psalm 2:7 says, *"I will declare the decree: the Lord hath said unto me, Thou art my Son; this day have I begotten thee."*

God holds His Word even above His name.

I'VE BEEN THERE BEFORE

Imagine for a moment you're an Israelite. You've been up against the Red Sea, with Pi-hahiroth and Migdol on one side of you, Baal-zephon behind you and the pursuing Egyptian army staring you in the face. There is nothing stretched out before you but the sea, and there you stood. Hearing the clanking and the clattering of the chariots of your adversary, you did not tuck tail and run.

When God said, "Go," you started wading out into the sea water with seaweed wrapping around your legs, believing in the natural that you were surely going to die. You thought you'd never make it to the other side. But you stood, and you kept on walking.

Now you have water up around your knees. Everybody's getting nervous. Everybody's saying, "Aren't you going to turn around?" But your faith goes back to when you were baking bricks. You can almost feel the lash of Pharaoh's whip upon your back. However, in your mind echoes the words of Yahweh, "I shall bring you out with a strong right arm." Now your hope is about to become faith!

Maybe you're in dire financial need. You've balanced your checking account. You've checked your calculator, torn up the ribbon and thrown it away. You've added up your money. But no matter how you look at it, it's still a bad report when you get to the bottom line.

Possibly you have been believing that your teenager was going to come out of the situation he or she was in. And, yet, on Friday night when your child comes home in a drunken stupor, you begin to wonder if things would ever change.

Everywhere you turn, you receive a bad report. And to make matters worse, it isn't even Sunday morning—where the preacher preaches a power-packed message, the organ plays, the choir sings, and thousands of people all add their faith to yours. It's just you now. It's the middle of the week, and trouble is closing in all around. There's no light anywhere. The darkness of your human experience beats upon you. There's no way you're going to make it.

Somehow, though, you stand in the middle of that darkness and raise your hands. You lift a voice that no one can hear but you. Be encouraged: you're not going in the wrong direction. You're going in the right direction. Even if you have no outward evidence, you have the illumination of His Word.

Jesus said it. So you can believe it.

God is a mighty refuge in the midst of the storms of your life. He is a strength, a strong tower, and a refuge. He will never allow you to sink in the billows of trials and tribulation.

As long as you zero in on God's Word, which cannot fail, the storms and the dark clouds may rise, but they won't worry you. You will receive your three-fold harvest. Why? Because you are sheltered, safe in the arms of God!

THE WORD SPEAKS

I was born in January in Cuyahoga County at St. Luke's Hospital, Cleveland, Ohio. There were 22 inches of snow on the ground.

Not far from our church, near the little town of Lithopolis, there are a lot of apple orchards. It's so beautiful in the winter, with a blanket of snow laying at the base of those beautiful apple trees, but they're stark. There are no leaves. There are no apples.

It would surely get my attention if, driving through row after row of those apple trees in January, with a blanket of white snow on the ground, I saw one of those apple trees hanging full of red, juicy, delicious apples. Because apple trees don't have apples on them in the middle of January. The elements—the cold, the wind, and the snow — won't allow it to bear fruit.

So it is with human existence. When it's winter in your life, and it's impossible for you to bear fruit, God said, "I will cause you to bear fruit in the middle of the winter."

Do you know what God is saying? If you're walking through the winter of your life and you take His word that He has declared unto you, mix it with faith in the generator of your spirit, when trouble all around is assailing you and you begin to praise Him, your words will become fruit. He'll see the fruit of your lips, run after His Word, and He will perform it.

DELEGATED AUTHORITY

You and I are in authority in this earth. We have delegated authority. According to Isaiah 55:11, God sent His Word, but it does not return to Him. Why? Because it is God's responsibility to send it, but it is *our* responsibility to return it back to Him.

It's as though God makes a deposit of His Word in you, just as you make a deposit in a bank. If I made a deposit in your bank account of $10,000, you will never drive the car that $10,000 could buy unless you learn how to make a withdrawal.

The Lord of Hosts makes a deposit of His Word in your spirit and expects you to access it and make a withdrawal with your faith through the confession of your mouth.

You are what you say—because out of the abundance of the heart, the mouth speaks. (See Luke 6:45.) And God establishes your word. But God said, "If you will release that word back, it will accomplish that for which I sent it."

I remember a time in my early years of preaching that I had to put a voice to my faith, and use my delegated authority.

I was scheduled to preach at another church when my vocal chords became swollen and began to bleed. At that time in my ministry I preached three Sunday services, a midweek service and several times on the road. But this night I was in terrible pain.

When I arrived in town I was unable to speak. But in my hotel room I opened my Bible, walked around the room and began pointing to it. I didn't do this for an hour or two. I did it continuously, all day long. I would mouth the words, "I believed I received when I prayed. I thank you, Lord, my vocal chords are strong. I will preach tonight like a man from another world."

I walked around the room mouthing the Word of God, but there was no sound. I would say things like Isaiah 53:5: *"But he was wounded for our transgressions, he was bruised for our iniquities: the chastisement of our peace was upon him; and with his stripes we are healed."*

When I arrived at the service that night, I went

through the entire praise and worship service, singing, but not a note was heard. But something happened. When I walked to the pulpit, the first thing I did was grab the microphone, opened up my mouth and said, "Praise the Lord, everybody." My voice was strong, and I preached until the people could hardly sit there.

Right now, you can make a decision. You can allow your mountain to move your faith, or you can allow your faith to move your mountain. The choice is yours.

I have discovered that if I believe in my heart and confess with my mouth, I can have whatever I say. Therefore when you pray, *believe* and you will receive.

Faith is not hard. You exercise faith every time you pray. You either believed you did, or you believed you didn't. You've just got to turn the switch in order to receive your harvest.

Chapter Four

ALL THINGS NEW

There's something special about a new beginning.

When a prisoner is pardoned, whether from the state governor or the President of the United States, something unique takes place. The man or woman who receives the pardon not only is released from jail, but also has the record of his or her wrongdoing erased. Officially, it's as though the prisoner's past has been wiped clean.

Forgiveness has new-beginning qualities as well. When we truly forgive someone who has wronged us, it's as though they stop living in our heads without paying rent! We don't have to pretend that what they did to us was okay or didn't hurt, but we give ourselves a new start—because we relinquish the control the past has over our actions.

We are living in an amazing time, when the public's attention is focused on the church in a way it's rarely been in my lifetime. It is a prime time for us to evangelize the lost, because the church is showing the heart and character of the God it serves. Our unsaved friends, family members and co-workers are increasingly interested in this God who loves you and Whom you love.

If you and I are faithful to witness His love to others, we will see the truth of these words of the apostle Paul: *"Therefore if any man be in Christ, he is a new creature: old things are passed away; behold, all things are become new" (2 Corinthians 5:17).*

We're living in the final days, when all things become new again!

Did you know that what's happening *in* you is greater than what is happening *to* you? God is about to do a brand-new thing! That means your old way of doing things is about to die, so God can resurrect it anew. The Lord wants to instill mountain-moving faith in your spirit, as Jesus did with his disciples:

And Jesus answering saith unto them, Have faith in God. For verily I say unto you, That whosoever shall say unto this mountain, Be thou removed, and be thou cast into the sea; and shall not doubt in his heart, but shall believe that those things which he saith shall come to pass; he shall have whatsoever he saith. Therefore I say unto you, What things soever ye desire, when ye pray, believe that ye receive them, and ye shall have them.

—Mark 11:22-24

How is He going to do it? Ephesians 3:20 says, *"Now unto him that is able to do exceeding abundantly above all that we ask or think, according to the power that worketh in us."*

God is able to save you from a life marked by lack! The Lord is about to deliver you from the chains of debt! God is able to save you from a mindset of poverty! God is able to place within you a new heart and a new spirit that is full of faith to believe for anything you need!

The prophet Ezekiel declares:

> *A new heart also will I give you, and a new spirit will I put within you: and I will take away the stony heart out of your flesh, and I will give you an heart of flesh. And I will put my spirit within you, and cause you to walk in my statutes, and ye shall keep my judgments, and do them. And ye shall dwell in the land that I gave to your fathers; and ye shall be my people, and I will be your God. I will also save you from all your uncleannesses: and I will call for the corn, and will increase it, and lay no famine upon you. And I will multiply the fruit of the tree, and the increase of the field, that ye shall receive no more reproach of famine among the heathen.*
> —*Ezekiel 36:26-30*

Do you remember when you were first saved? Everything seemed brighter. Everyone seemed happier. Your body felt better. It probably seemed to you like nothing would ever go wrong in your life again. I believe the Lord is about to put a new anointing on you—an anointing that will remind you of when you were first saved. You'll be like someone who doesn't want to wake up from a wonderful dream, because the blessing of God will be so rich upon your life.

The psalmist wrote,

> *When the Lord turned again the captivity of Zion, we were like them that dream. Then was our mouth filled with laughter, and our tongue with singing: then said they among the heathen, The Lord hath done great things for them. The Lord hath done great things for us; whereof we are glad.*
>
> *—Psalm 126:1-3*

Like the people the psalmist referred to, you will laugh and sing with joy as you discover what God has *already* prepared to bless you!

A New Thing

Not long ago, God gave me a very specific word originally declared by the prophet, Isaiah:

Sing, O barren, thou that didst not bear; break forth into singing, and cry aloud, thou that didst not travail with child: for more are the children of the desolate than the children of the married wife, saith the Lord. Enlarge the place of thy tent, and let them stretch forth the curtains of thine habitations: spare not, lengthen thy cords, and strengthen thy stakes; For thou shalt break forth on the right hand and on the left; and thy seed shall inherit the Gentiles, and make the desolate cities to be inhabited. Fear not; for thou shalt not be ashamed: neither be thou confounded; for thou shalt not be put to shame: for thou shalt forget the shame of thy youth, and shalt not remember the reproach of thy widowhood any more. For thy Maker is thine husband; the Lord of hosts is his

*name; and thy Redeemer the Holy One of
Israel; The God of the whole earth shall he
be called. For the Lord hath called thee as
a woman forsaken and grieved in spirit,
and a wife of youth, when thou wast
refused, saith thy God. For a small moment
have I forsaken thee; but with great mercies will I gather thee. In a little wrath I hid
my face from thee for a moment; but with
everlasting kindness will I have mercy on
thee, saith the Lord thy Redeemer.*

—Isaiah 54:1-8

God is telling us to prepare for increase in our
life, because *it's already there.* As we obey him and
advance the kingdom of God in our circles of influ-
ence, He is planning to reward us for our obedience!

In order to build upon our faith, it's important
for us to remember what God did for us in the past.
David declared,

*Bless the Lord, O my soul: and all that
is within me, bless his holy name. Bless the*

Lord, O my soul, and forget not all his benefits: Who forgiveth all thine iniquities; who healeth all thy diseases; Who redeemeth thy life from destruction; who crowneth thee with lovingkindness and tender mercies; Who satisfieth thy mouth with good things; so that thy youth is renewed like the eagle's.

—Psalm 103:1-5

Jehovah Nissi, the Lord our banner of victory, doesn't want us to forget the victories He has won on our behalf. But He has *new* victories and fresh mercies awaiting us in the land of harvest.

The prophet Jeremiah stated,

It is of the Lord's mercies that we are not consumed, because his compassions fail not. They are new every morning: great is thy faithfulness.

—Lamentations 3:22,23

Jehovah wrought a wonderful work when He led the Israelites through the Red Sea as they fled their taskmasters' bondage. What became a passage for them became a barrier for the Egyptians. The Red Sea was a source of safety to the Israelites, but it quickly became a stumbling block to their enemies. The water became a refuge and a road to God's chosen people, but was a grave for the Egyptians.

After passing through the Red Sea, the Israelites then made their way to Canaan through a dry, parched desert land. And still God sustained them. He who made a way in the sea can also make a way in the wilderness. He who made dry land of the Red Sea could, and did, make dry land of the Jordan River.

God made a way where there was no way. I like to say it this way: where there is a will, there is a way!

So many times our miracle is dependent upon knowing the will of our Heavenly Father. Jesus left us His last will and testament through His inspired Word, which we revere today as the Bible. But often we don't take the time to discover the will of God for our lives. And that grieves the heart of God.

We are commanded to read the Bible and use it to discern God's will. Jesus admonished,

> *Search the scriptures; for in them ye think ye have eternal life: and they are they which testify of me. And ye will not come to me, that ye might have life. I receive not honour from men. But I know you, that ye have not the love of God in you. I am come in my Father's name, and ye receive me not: if another shall come in his own name, him ye will receive. How can ye believe, which receive honour one of another, and seek not the honour that cometh from God only? Do not think that I will accuse you to the Father: there is one that accuseth you, even Moses, in whom ye trust. For had ye believed Moses, ye would have believed me: for he wrote of me. But if ye believe not his writings, how shall ye believe my words?*
>
> —John 5:39-47

In order to perpetuate the will of God in our

family, health, and finances, we must ask Him for what we need.

First John 5:14 states, *"And this is the confidence that we have in him, that, if we ask any thing according to his will, he heareth us."*

I believe many people misinterpret this verse. They believe it means that if we ask anything according to God's will, *only then* will he hear us. But I believe what the Holy Spirit is *really* saying is that if we ask anything, God's will is to hear and answer us.

How many times have you prayed, "If it be Thy will, help me get out of debt. If it be Thy will, help me to have more than enough to meet my needs." Friend, I have good news for you! You don't have to wonder "if" your prosperity is God's will! When we discover the will of God, according to His Word, we will understand that He *desires* for us to prosper. Our prosperity is *already there*. We just need to ask for it in faith. In another of his letters, the apostle John wrote,

Beloved, I wish above all things that thou mayest prosper and be in health, even

as thy soul prospereth. For I rejoiced greatly, when the brethren came and testified of the truth that is in thee, even as thou walkest in the truth. I have no greater joy than to hear that my children walk in truth.
—*3 John 2-4*

GOD'S NEW THING SPRINGS FORTH

The prophet Isaiah wrote,

Thus saith the Lord, which maketh a way in the sea, and a path in the mighty waters; Which bringeth forth the chariot and horse, the army and the power; they shall lie down together, they shall not rise: they are extinct, they are quenched as tow. Remember ye not the former things, neither consider the things of old. Behold, I will do a new thing; now it shall spring forth; shall ye not know it? I will even make a way in the wilderness, and rivers in the desert.

—*Isaiah 43:16-19*

The new thing God is about to do shall spring forth *now*! You don't have to wait for the reward of your obedience any longer! It's *already there*! It's in the field, just waiting for you to put your sickle in and reap!

So many Christians have taken the bypass to their harvest. They've waited and waited, believing that *someday* it will happen. I'm here to tell you that the time is now and *this* is the day!

THIRD-DAY CHRISTIANS

My friends, I believe that you've been waiting for the rewards of your obedience long enough. It's time to ask for it in faith! It's time for you to possess your promised harvest in every area of your life!

This is the year when you are on your way out of the wilderness and into the land of Canaan to reap your promised harvest!

The prophet Hosea wrote,

> *Come, and let us return unto the Lord:*
> *for he hath torn, and he will heal us; he*

hath smitten, and he will bind us up. After two days will he revive us: in the third day he will raise us up, and we shall live in his sight. Then shall we know, if we follow on to know the Lord: his going forth is prepared as the morning; and he shall come unto us as the rain, as the latter and former rain unto the earth.

—Hosea 6:1-3

I believe the Lord showed me that we have just now entered what Hosea refers to as the third day. We are living in a time when old things pass away and all things become new!

The third day represents resurrection day. It was the third day when Jesus kicked the stone out of a borrowed tomb and rose again as our Savior and Canaan King. It was the third day that Joshua was told to cross the Jordan River.

We're getting ready to bury our past and resurrect a new beginning in every area of our lives! We're living in a time where wanderers become conquerors!

You are not just going to conquer your unclaimed riches in your life. You are going to reap a harvest in your family as well! It's a new day for a new church, full of new believers, with a new song, with a new shout, and a new word.

God is about to push you over the edge into your harvest! It's time to get up. It's time to go. It's time to go get what belongs to us.

JUST DO IT!

Do you know what the first step is to reaping your harvest? The answer is found in the account of Jesus's first miracle:

> *And the third day there was a marriage in Cana of Galilee; and the mother of Jesus was there: And both Jesus was called, and his disciples, to the marriage. And when they wanted wine, the mother of Jesus saith unto him, They have no wine. Jesus saith unto her, Woman, what have I to do with thee? mine hour is not yet come.*

His mother saith unto the servants, Whatsoever he saith unto you, do it. And there were set there six waterpots of stone, after the manner of the purifying of the Jews, containing two or three firkins apiece. Jesus saith unto them, Fill the waterpots with water. And they filled them up to the brim. And he saith unto them, Draw out now, and bear unto the governor of the feast. And they bare it. When the ruler of the feast had tasted the water that was made wine, and knew not whence it was: (but the servants which drew the water knew;) the governor of the feast called the bridegroom, And saith unto him, Every man at the beginning doth set forth good wine; and when men have well drunk, then that which is worse: but thou hast kept the good wine until now. This beginning of miracles did Jesus in Cana of Galilee, and manifested forth his glory; and his disciples believed on him.

—John 2:1-11

I don't know if the Nike sporting goods company borrowed its slogan from this passage. But you can adopt it as your own. If you want to receive what is already there for you, *just do it*. In other words, *obey God*!

The first step to reaping your harvest is, whatsoever the Holy Spirit is saying unto you, *do it*! Obeying God isn't always easy. But it is always worth it.

JESUS IS LOOKING FOR YOU!

Jesus is looking for some third-day Christians who are ready to march forward and possess what God has said is already there for them! Make no mistake about it—God will have a day. He will have an hour. God will have a moment when His church, full of His power, will stand in complete authority upon the face of this earth.

My questions to you are, "Why not *you*? Why not *here*? Why not *now*?"

We don't have to wait for everybody to get saved first. On the day of Pentecost about 120 believers gathered together in the Upper Room and received the Holy Spirit through a mighty rush of wind. So, it doesn't take many. Give me a band of believers who, possessed by the Holy Spirit, hate nothing but sin and love nothing but God.

I don't care whether they be preachers, clergy, or laity. Whoever is sold out to obey God no matter what will storm the gates of Hell, lift up their hands and declare, *"Thy kingdom come, Thy will be done in earth, as it is in heaven" (Matthew 6:10)*.

Have you seized the walled cities? Have you stared the giants of your life down in utter defiance? Our great leader and liberator, the Lord Jesus Christ, is sifting through the ranks of the self-indulgent and the self-   satisfied.

Deep within my spirit, I believe you're about to give birth to a miracle you didn't even know was in your belly. A harvest is waiting for you on the other side of Jordan's banks. But first you must prepare to leave the wilderness.

Chapter Five

CONQUERING FEAR AND GREED

Before we can truly possess our Promised Land, I believe it's important for you and me to understand why many Christians do not receive what God has prepared for them.

The greatest factors that will keep you wandering in the wilderness are *fear* and *greed*. These obstacles kept the first generation of Israelites from entering their Promised Land.

OVERCOMING THE SPIRIT OF FEAR

You've probably seen the acrostic that defines "fear." It is "**F**alse **E**vidence that **A**ppears **R**eal!"

Jesus said that man's fear would be a sign of his return to earth:

> *And when ye shall see Jerusalem compassed with armies, then know that the*

desolation thereof is nigh. Then let them which are in Judaea flee to the mountains; and let them which are in the midst of it depart out; and let not them that are in the countries enter thereinto. For these be the days of vengeance, that all things which are written may be fulfilled. But woe unto them that are with child, and to them that give suck, in those days! for there shall be great distress in the land, and wrath upon this people. And they shall fall by the edge of the sword, and shall be led away captive into all nations: and Jerusalem shall be trodden down of the Gentiles, until the times of the Gentiles be fulfilled.

—Luke 21:20-24

What do men and women fear? Anything and everything! They fear the economy, failure, or some impending financial crisis. The enemy would like nothing more than to grip your heart with fear and paralyze you, so you're unable to fulfill the call of God upon your life. In fact, your greatest opposition will *always* come right before your greatest breakthrough! Here's an example:

Before Moses died and Joshua arose in leader-
ship, prior to entering the Promised Land, the land
flowing with milk and honey, Moses sent twelve
spies to get the lay of the land. Ten of them returned
with an evil report. But two of them, Joshua and
Caleb, returned with a proclamation of promise and
blessing.

> *And Joshua the son of Nun, and Caleb
> the son of Jephunneh, which were of them
> that searched the land, rent their clothes:
> And they spake unto all the company of the
> children of Israel, saying, The land, which
> we passed through to search it, is an
> exceeding good land. If the Lord delight in
> us, then he will bring us into this land, and
> give it us; a land which floweth with milk
> and honey. Only rebel not ye against the
> Lord, neither fear ye the people of the
> land; for they are bread for us: their
> defence is departed from them, and the
> Lord is with us: fear them not. But all the
> congregation bade stone them with stones.*

And the glory of the Lord appeared in the tabernacle of the congregation before all the children of Israel.
—Numbers 14:6-10

We shouldn't be too hard on the children of Israel. They only did what we would do today. Unfortunately, then as now, the popular opinion was to stay back in the "Land of Just Enough," because of the fear of the unknown. Fear is the opposite of faith. Fear will paralyze the operation of the blessing of God in your life!

If the children of Israel had remembered that Joshua wanted to take them into the Promised Land, they wouldn't have been paralyzed by fear!

Provision prophesies provision. Supply is a prophetic indication of future supply! Victory in the past is a prophetic indicator of victory in the future! Unfortunately, many Christians today live in what I call the "Someday Syndrome." They think, "Well, *someday* I will have more than enough. *Someday* I will be healed. *Someday* I will walk in the blessing of God."

Friend, I have news for you. As long as you passively wait for it, "someday" will never come. The apostle Paul wrote,

> *For he saith, I have heard thee in a time accepted, and in the day of salvation have I succoured thee: behold, now is the accepted time; behold, now is the day of salvation.*
>
> —*2 Corinthians 6:2*

The fearful cannot strike a heavy blow in the hour of conflict. Fear paralyzes the arm, because it unnerves the heart. But men who are possessed by the Holy Spirit don't seek deliverance from the fires of adversity, nor do they petition the courts of heaven for tasks equal to their powers. Rather, they plead upon their knees for power that is equal to their task.

You and I need to have the courage to pro-claim, "Today, I enter the land. Today, the promise is mine. Today, I have more than enough! I refuse ever to be comfortable with lack again!" When we eliminate fear from our lives, we will see that our blessing from God is simply waiting for us to claim it. *It's already there.*

WITHHOLDING GOD'S PORTION

The second reason people do not sow seed is greed. Too many Christians are greedy, withholding what God has given them to hoard for themselves. And incredibly, the One they withhold from is God Himself!

The book of Proverbs proclaims:

Honour the Lord with thy substance, and with the firstfruits of all thine increase: So shall thy barns be filled with plenty, and thy presses shall burst out with new wine.

—Proverbs 3:9,10

When you honor God as He is to be honored—when you eliminate greed from your life—an amazing thing happens. The apostle Paul wrote, *"For if the firstfruit be holy, the lump is also holy:*

and if the root be holy, so are the branches"
(Romans 11:16).

What is God saying in this verse? He's telling you to sanctify, or set apart, your finances unto Him. If you will sanctify your firstfruits unto him, the whole will be sanctified. And the whole is *everything that pertains to you!* Everything in your life is to be set apart unto Him!

If you earn $100 and obediently bring a crisp, new $10 bill to the Lord as His tithe, then that tithe is not an ordinary piece of currency—anymore than the rod of Moses was an ordinary stick, or the mantle of Elijah was an ordinary piece of cloth. The Lord has already earmarked your tithe. It's as if He folded the corner down and said, "This one's mine." Therefore, it has miracle-working power. When God touches that piece of paper in your hand, He can multiply it until a mountain of obligations disappears. Stretch forth your seed over the distress of your life and watch your miracle begin. The Lord will part the waters of debt and distress, and you'll walk on dry ground.

THE GOLDEN GOBLETS

Another example of man's wrongly using that which is sanctified unto the Lord is found in the book of Daniel:

But hast lifted up thyself against the Lord of heaven; and they have brought the vessels of his house before thee, and thou, and thy lords, thy wives, and thy concubines, have drunk wine in them; and thou hast praised the gods of silver, and gold, of brass, iron, wood, and stone, which see not, nor hear, nor know: and the God in whose hand thy breath is, and whose are all thy ways, hast thou not glorified: Then was the part of the hand sent from him; and this writing was written.

And this is the writing that was written, MENE, MENE, TEKEL, UPHARSIN. This is the interpretation of the thing: Mene; God hath numbered thy kingdom, and finished it. Tekel; Thou art weighed in

the balances, and art found wanting.
—Daniel 5:23-27

Belshazzar used the golden goblets, sanctified to God, for a profane use. Therefore, he was weighed in the balance and found wanting. His enemies invaded the land because he opened the door to the devil through his disobedience. Then the river dried up.

In our day, the river is symbolic of the Holy Spirit. When disobedience is present, the move of God in our life is quenched. Then we lack both provision and supply.

Belshazzar died as a result of his disobedience. How often have we allowed our harvest to die on the vine or rot in the field because of our disobedience? The good news is, it doesn't have to be that way!

It's time to change our minds. It's time to be obedient in *every* area of our lives! It's time to put away greed!

OBEDIENCE IS BETTER THAN SACRIFICE

Israel's first king, Saul, is yet another illustration of how greed can cause judgment to come upon a people.

> *And Saul said unto Samuel, Yea, I have obeyed the voice of the Lord, and have gone the way which the Lord sent me, and have brought Agag the king of Amalek, and have utterly destroyed the Amalekites. But the people took of the spoil, sheep and oxen, the chief of the things which should have been utterly destroyed, to sacrifice unto the Lord thy God in Gilgal. And Samuel said, Hath the Lord as great delight in burnt offerings and sacrifices, as in obeying the voice of the Lord? Behold, to obey is better than sacrifice, and to hearken than the fat of rams. For rebellion is as the sin of witchcraft, and stubbornness is as iniquity and idolatry. Because thou hast rejected the word of the Lord, he*

hath also rejected thee from being king.
            — 1 Samuel 15:20-23

Saul was disobedient in many ways. He did not destroy the spoils of war. And he disobeyed the voice of the prophet. As a result, his kingdom was taken from him.

Disobedience can cause your blessing to be forfeited. It opens the door for the devil. And it can cut off your source of help. Fortunately, we can choose, through obedience, to sanctify the Lord on the inside of us. As we do so, our seed is sanctified.

You and I must decide not to use God's property for anything other than what He intends for it to be used. We are kingdom people. We don't need position or popularity. We don't need a pat on the back. We don't cave in when the going gets rough. We are happy to be in the battle. We are kingdom people who are tired of status quo Christianity. We are tired of not having enough to make ends meet. We are tired of sickness in our bodies. Like an army with banners, we are crossing Jordan to possess the land. We will stand with our feet firmly planted in our Promised Land and proclaim that a genuine, culture-shaking financial revolution is underway. We will take this kingdom by force!

Chapter Six

HONORING THE KING

God delights in memorials. Throughout the Bible, He admonished His people, "Everywhere you go, build an altar there, to remember that that's where you met Me."

After the Israelites crossed the Jordan River, they built a memorial to the Lord to remember their deliverance into the Promised Land:

> *And it came to pass, when all the people were clean passed over Jordan, that the Lord spake unto Joshua, saying, Take you twelve men out of the people, out of every tribe a man, And command ye them, saying, Take you hence out of the midst of Jordan, out of the place where the priests' feet stood firm, twelve stones, and ye shall carry them over with you, and leave them in the lodging place, where ye shall lodge*

this night. Then Joshua called the twelve men, whom he had prepared of the children of Israel, out of every tribe a man: And Joshua said unto them, Pass over before the ark of the Lord your God into the midst of Jordan, and take ye up every man of you a stone upon his shoulder, according unto the number of the tribes of the children of Israel: That this may be a sign among you, that when your children ask their fathers in time to come, saying, What mean ye by these stones? Then ye shall answer them, That the waters of Jordan were cut off before the ark of the covenant of the Lord; when it passed over Jordan, the waters of Jordan were cut off: and these stones shall be for a memorial unto the children of Israel for ever.

—*Joshua 4:1-7*

What is a memorial? The International Standard Bible Encyclopedia defines a memorial as "a sacrificial term, that which brings the offerer into remembrance before God, or brings God into favorable remembrance with the offerer."

There are many other examples of memorials given throughout the Bible. They were all designed to honor God.

A PROPHET IS BORN

Hannah knew about memorials. She was one of two wives married to Elkanah. However, she was barren.

Every year, Elkanah and his wives went to the temple to worship God. During this time, Elkanah's second wife, Peninnah, provoked Hannah because she was barren. Therefore, she wept before the Lord:

> *So Hannah rose up after they had eaten in Shiloh, and after they had drunk. Now Eli the priest sat upon a seat by a post of the temple of the Lord. And she was in bitterness of soul, and prayed unto the Lord, and wept sore. And she vowed a vow, and said, O Lord of hosts, if thou wilt*

indeed look on the affliction of thine hand-maid, and remember me, and not forget thine handmaid, but wilt give unto thine handmaid a man child, then I will give him unto the Lord all the days of his life, and there shall no razor come upon his head. And it came to pass, as she continued pray-ing before the Lord, that Eli marked her mouth. Now Hannah, she spake in her heart; only her lips moved, but her voice was not heard: therefore Eli thought she had been drunken. And Eli said unto her, How long wilt thou be drunken? put away thy wine from thee. And Hannah answered and said, No, my lord, I am a woman of a sorrowful spirit: I have drunk neither wine nor strong drink, but have poured out my soul before the Lord. Count not thine hand-maid for a daughter of Belial: for out of the abundance of my complaint and grief have I spoken hitherto. Then Eli answered and said, Go in peace: and the God of Israel grant thee thy petition that thou hast asked of him. And she said, Let thine handmaid

*find grace in thy sight. So the woman went
her way, and did eat, and her countenance
was no more sad. And they rose up in the
morning early, and worshipped before the
Lord, and returned, and came to their
house to Ramah: and Elkanah knew
Hannah his wife; and the Lord remembered her.*

— 1 Samuel 1:9-19

Hannah cried out to God in the temple for a
child. She mixed her praying with her giving. Her
prayer went up as a memorial before God and he
gave her the prophet, Samuel. Not only did she
give birth to one of Israel's greatest prophets, the
Lord gave her six more children!

A MEMORIAL BRINGS ABOUT VICTORY

Jephthah, the son of Gilead, was familiar with
memorials:

*Then the Spirit of the Lord came upon
Jephthah, and he passed over Gilead, and*

Manasseh, and passed over Mizpeh of Gilead, and from Mizpeh of Gilead he passed over unto the children of Ammon. And Jephthah vowed a vow unto the Lord, and said, If thou shalt without fail deliver the children of Ammon into mine hands, Then it shall be, that whatsoever cometh forth of the doors of my house to meet me, when I return in peace from the children of Ammon, shall surely be the Lord's, and I will offer it up for a burnt offering.

So Jephthah passed over unto the children of Ammon to fight against them; and the Lord delivered them into his hands. And he smote them from Aroer, even till thou come to Minnith, even twenty cities, and unto the plain of the vineyards, with a very great slaughter. Thus the children of Ammon were subdued before the children of Israel.

And Jephthah came to Mizpeh unto his house, and, behold, his daughter came out

*to meet him with timbrels and with dances:
and she was his only child; beside her he
had neither son nor daughter. And it came
to pass, when he saw her, that he rent his
clothes, and said, Alas, my daughter! thou
hast brought me very low, and thou art one
of them that trouble me: for I have opened
my mouth unto the Lord, and I cannot go
back.*

—Judges 11:29-35

Jephthah was a desperate man. His prayer before God was a matter of life and death. He reached deep within himself and found the kind of prayer that gets God's attention immediately—the prayer mixed with giving, because giving is an act of faith.

Jephthah told the Lord if He would give him the victory over the Ammonites, He would give him the first thing that came through his door. More than 40,000 men were slaughtered that day, and God secured Israel's victory because of the prayer of Jephthah.

A HOUSEHOLD IS SAVED

Cornelius, a centurion, dedicated his life to mixing his praying with his giving:

> *There was a certain man in Caesarea called Cornelius, a centurion of the band called the Italian band, A devout man, and one that feared God with all his house, which gave much alms to the people, and prayed to God alway. He saw in a vision evidently about the ninth hour of the day an angel of God coming in to him, and saying unto him, Cornelius. And when he looked on him, he was afraid, and said, What is it, Lord? And he said unto him, Thy prayers and thine alms are come up for a memorial before God.*
>
> *—Acts 10:1-4*

The Bible called Cornelius a devout man—one who feared God. God said that the centurion's prayers and his alms had come up as a memorial before Him. Therefore, He prepared Peter to show

Cornelius the way of salvation. As a result, the centurion's entire household was saved.

PRAYER MIXED WITH GIVING

In all of these instances, men and women wrapped their faith with their life. In all of those examples, they mixed their praying and their giving. They targeted their seed toward their need.

In each instance, God's response was essentially, "I must know where your heart is in regard to your prayer. When I see your sacrifice following that prayer, I know that where your treasure is, there your heart is also."

Memorials are central to our lives. They help us remember all God has done for us, and to appropriately honor Him each day. A memorial sets a mark upon your prayer. When you use memorials in your life effectively, you'll never forget that it's Jehovah Jireh, your Provider, which has made a way through the wilderness and a river in the desert.

I want to encourage you to set memorials in

your life as a testimony to what God has done for you. They can greatly improve your prayer life and, in turn, your relationship with the Almighty. They can be simple things—a cross you carry in your pocket, a picture that reminds you of a difficult time God brought you through, or something else. The substance of the memorial is far less important than the action it inspires in you. A good memorial should inspire your praise to God and your obedience to Him.

There are many milestones in your life as you walk with God. May God help us not to be like the lepers, whom Jesus healed, but who never came back and said, "Thank you for cleansing me."

That is what the Israelites remembered. They remembered that it was God alone who provided a way for them to cross over. However, now was not the time to quit. God was just beginning to move in a miraculous way. Now it was time to possess the Promised Land.

Chapter Seven

PROTECTING WHAT'S PROMISED

Once the last memorial had been built on the shore of their new homeland, God commanded the Israelites to possess the land. He told Joshua:

> *Pass through the host, and command the people, saying, Prepare you victuals; for within three days ye shall pass over this Jordan, to go in to possess the land, which the Lord your God giveth you to possess it.*
> —*Joshua 1:11*

The word "possess" is a war term. It means to drive out and spoil the previous tenants. Israel was commanded to defeat its enemies and, through God's provision, the enemies would be driven from the land.

However, did you ever wonder why the Lord brought the Israelites over the Jordan at the time when the snow was melting and the river was over-flowing its banks?

As I said earlier, the manna had ceased. Therefore, Israel would need food, clothing, and shelter once they passed over into the land of Canaan.

The children of Israel were told to cross over during the time when the early harvest was ripening throughout the country. The corn was in the land ready to be reaped! Their sustenance was waiting for them.

Suppose there had been no corn in the fields ready for reaping. How would the children of Israel have been fed when they were across the river? Remember that the manna, the sustenance the children of Israel had become accustomed to, had ceased.

OUT OF THE HOUSE OF BONDAGE

When the Israelites took possession of Canaan, it was already furnished for their habitation. Cities were built and houses were furnished for their use. Wells were dug from which to fetch water. The vineyards were ready to be consumed. The ground was already cultivated. Everything Israel needed was already there. They just had to be obedient to God's commands.

God was about to fulfill the promise He had made to His servant, Moses, when He first brought the children of Israel out of the land of Egypt:

> *And it shall be, when the Lord thy God shall have brought thee into the land which he sware unto thy fathers, to Abraham, to Isaac, and to Jacob, to give thee great and goodly cities, which thou buildedst not, And houses full of all good things, which thou filledst not, and wells digged, which thou diggedst not, vineyards and olive trees, which thou plantedst not; when thou shalt have eaten and be full; Then beware lest thou forget the Lord, which brought thee forth out of the land of Egypt, from the house of bondage.*
>
> *—Deuteronomy 6:10-12*

When the Israelites left Egypt, the house of bondage, they were laden with the country's wealth. Notwithstanding, for 40 years, despite their disobedience, God performed the miraculous so that their shoes and clothes never wore out; manna fell daily from heaven, and water flowed freely from a rock.

God supernaturally sustained Israel. Nevertheless, when they possessed the Promised Land, they owned none of the land. They couldn't trace their ownership through their ancestors.

They owed *everything* to the goodness of God. For it was God who had given them the land. Likewise, we owe our possessions to God, *"For the Lord God is a sun and shield: the Lord will give grace and glory: no good thing will he withhold from them that walk uprightly"* *(Psalm 84:11)*.

A PROMISE BECOMES A REALITY

Joshua reminded them of the promise when it had become a reality, and the Israelites responded appropriately:

And I have given you a land for which ye did not labour, and cities which ye built not, and ye dwell in them; of the vineyards and oliveyards which ye planted not do ye eat. Now therefore fear the Lord, and serve him in sincerity and in truth: and put away the gods which your fathers served on the other side of the flood, and in Egypt; and serve ye the Lord. And if it seem evil unto you to serve the Lord, choose you this day whom ye will serve; whether the gods which your fathers served that were on the other side of the flood, or the gods of the Amorites, in whose land ye dwell: but as for me and my house, we will serve the Lord. And the people answered and said, God forbid that we should forsake the Lord, to serve other gods; For the Lord our God, he it is that brought us up and our fathers out of the land of Egypt, from the house of bondage, and which did those great signs in our sight, and preserved us in all the way wherein we went, and among all the people through whom we passed:

And the Lord drave out from before us all the people, even the Amorites which dwelt in the land: therefore will we also serve the Lord; for he is our God. And Joshua said unto the people, Ye cannot serve the Lord: for he is an holy God; he is a jealous God; he will not forgive your transgressions nor your sins. If ye forsake the Lord, and serve strange gods, then he will turn and do you hurt, and consume you, after that he hath done you good. And the people said unto Joshua, Nay; but we will serve the Lord. And Joshua said unto the people, Ye are witnesses against yourselves that ye have chosen you the Lord, to serve him. And they said, We are witnesses. Now therefore put away, said he, the strange gods which are among you, and incline your heart unto the Lord God of Israel. And the people said unto Joshua, The Lord our God will we serve, and his voice will we obey.

—Joshua 24:13-24

Israel committed not to forget the Lord God who brought them out of the land of Egypt. Every piece of food, provision of crops and portion of land was a reminder to the Israelite that the Lord brought them into the land of plenty from the house of bondage. Every grape was a reminder of God's provision. Every handful of grain was a token to the Lord's supply. Every well was a memorial that they would no longer drink from a rock, but from the rains of heaven.

DWELLING IN THE LAND OF PROMISES

God caused Israel's adversaries to prepare a great reception for their entry into their new homeland. A grand banquet waited for them in the fields. They had possessed their Promised Land, and now it was time to dwell there:

"And it shall be, when thou art come in unto the land which the Lord thy God giveth thee for an inheritance, and possessest it, and dwellest therein" (Deuteronomy 26:1).

The children of Israel were to protect the land

by physically dwelling in it and becoming long-term residents. The Hebrew word for "dwell" in Deuteronomy 26:1 is *yashab*—which means "to settle into," or "to be secure" or "abide."

It refers to the place where you homestead, marry, set up housekeeping and resist all "claim jumpers." To homestead required that one prove his right of ownership by fencing it in.

They were also charged to continue to sow crops and dig wells in the land. The Lord provides not only provision, but also protection. He has placed us in a position of absolute protection, under His care.

The Psalmist wrote,

He that dwelleth in the secret place of the most High shall abide under the shadow of the Almighty. I will say of the Lord, He is my refuge and my fortress: my God; in him will I trust. Surely he shall deliver thee from the snare of the fowler, and from the noisome pestilence. He shall cover thee with his feathers, and under his wings shalt thou trust: his truth shall be thy shield and

buckler. Thou shalt not be afraid for the terror by night; nor for the arrow that flieth by day; Nor for the pestilence that walketh in darkness; nor for the destruction that wasteth at noonday. A thousand shall fall at thy side, and ten thousand at thy right hand; but it shall not come nigh thee. Only with thine eyes shalt thou behold and see the reward of the wicked.
—Psalm 91:1-8

God will drive off those who would steal the seeds from the land you possess and protect your field from intruders. We must resist *all* claim jumpers!

God told the Israelites to mark the land with a claim to ownership by sowing seed. When you sow a seed toward your greatest need—whether it's your marriage, your children, your finances or your health—you're telling the enemy that area of your life is *off limits* to him!

TREASURES WORTH POSSESSING

The Israelites, dwelling in the land of plenty, felt indebted to God—and appropriately so. It's also appropriate for you and I to pay homage to Him who gave us His only Son:

For God so loved the world, that he gave his only begotten Son, that whosoever believeth in him should not perish, but have everlasting life. For God sent not his Son into the world to condemn the world; but that the world through him might be saved. He that believeth on him is not condemned: but he that believeth not is condemned already, because he hath not believed in the name of the only begotten Son of God.

—John 3:16-18

In light of our Lord's supreme sacrifice on our behalf, let us offer unto God our best offering. Let us start what He has finished. Let us, in deep humility, set our heart upon God as our eyes look across the Jordan River. For our Lord, in His grace and goodness, has prepared for us a harvest worth possessing.

May our prayer mirror that of the old hymn that says, "On Jordan's stormy banks I stand, and cast a wishful eye. To Canaan's fair and happy land, where my possessions lie!"

IT'S ALREADY THERE

Chapter Eight

TIME TO REAP

The Israelites had successfully crossed over the Jordan River and possessed the land. Now it was time to put in the sickle and reap their harvest! They had obeyed—now it was time to claim what God had already provided for them!

The Lord brought His people to Jordan at the time when the snow was melting on Lebanon. The river was overflowing.

The harvest was coming to maturity in every field throughout the land. Their crops stood in the fields, ready to be gathered. Their cities were already built. The homes were already furnished! God had already provided everything the children of Israel would need to inhabit the land!

God's chosen people were prepared to possess the land, and they did. The hand of God's favor was upon them. They were called and anointed for such a time as this!

THUS SAYS THE LORD TO HIS ANOINTED

One of the greatest barometers which distinguishes our generation in the last days is this: God has begun to pour out revelation upon revelation, truth upon truth, line upon line, precept upon precept to become the building stones for us to climb out of the dungeons of poverty and lack. For too long, the church has sat on the sidelines, believing that *someday* she will walk in the blessing of God. But I have a word for you that refutes the whole notion of "someday"! It's found in Isaiah 45:1:

> *Thus saith the Lord to his anointed, to Cyrus, whose right hand I have holden, to subdue nations before him; and I will loose the loins of kings, to open before him the two leaved gates; and the gates shall not be shut.*

Notice the word "anointed." Here Isaiah is referring to the pagan king, Cyrus. Some 150 years before he was born, Isaiah began to prophesy about this deliverer of the Jewish people.

Cyrus did not serve Jehovah. But God announced, through Isaiah, that he was anointed? Why? Because the Lord was going to use him to bring His people back to their own land.

Do you know what "anointed" means? It means to be painted, like a target, with a fragrance that attracts the favor of God. As a blood-bought believer in Jesus Christ, *you* are anointed, or painted, with a fragrance that attracts the favor of God.

The prophet continued:

I will go before thee, and make the crooked places straight: I will break in pieces the gates of brass, and cut in sunder the bars of iron: And I will give thee the treasures of darkness, and hidden riches of secret places, that thou mayest know that I, the Lord, which call thee by thy name, am the God of Israel. For Jacob my servant's sake, and Israel mine elect, I have even called thee by thy name: I have surnamed thee, though thou hast not known me. I am the Lord, and there is none else, there is no God beside me: I girded thee, though thou hast not known me: That they may know from the rising of the sun, and from the west, that there is none beside me. I am the Lord, and there is none else. I form the light, and create darkness: I make peace, and create evil: I the Lord do all these things.

—Isaiah 45:2-7

God wants you to know that your harvest is *already there*, waiting for you in the fields. It may have been covered up. But the light of His Word is about to reveal those *treasures of darkness and hidden riches of secret places!*

There is coming a time in the body of Christ when the reapers are going to overtake the sowers. This means there is coming a time when you are going to put in the seed with one hand—and before it can hit the ground, with the other hand you're going to reap. Faster than you can get your seed sown, you'll be taking it out.

You're living in the time when your harvest is already in the field! God is just waiting on you to reap!

Let me tell you something else: you're not only going to reap where you sow. You're also going to reap where you *didn't* sow. And you are going to reap in some unusual places.

God is going to invade your everyday life with a harvest. He wants to prove to you that He alone is the Lord. He *will* show up, regardless of what you have done or what you are expecting. That's what the anointing is about. It's the perpetual propulsion of the energy of God which will propel you through every line of opposition the world has to offer!

Like Joshua and the children of Israel, we are trespassing into enemy-held territory. God is going to shower us with a great downpour of blessing— so much that we will have enough left over to help finance the spread of the Gospel to lost and hurting humanity!

THE WEALTH OF THE WORLD

I want you to understand that at this moment in time, it's our covenant right to go get our promised harvest. The wealth the world has laid up belongs to us.

Proverbs 13:22 declares, *"A good man leaveth an inheritance to his children's children: and the wealth of the sinner is laid up for the just."*

We're going to invade enemy-held territory, and all along the way God is just going to drop some blessings for you to pick up. It's time to start walking around in the atmosphere of expectancy. The adversary has walked into your life and your home and stolen from you. But we are about to take back everything he has stolen!

The book of Proverbs says,

> *Men do not despise a thief, if he steal to satisfy his soul when he is hungry; But if he be found, he shall restore sevenfold; he shall give all the substance of his house.*
> —*Proverbs 6:30,31*

AN IMMEDIATE HARVEST

The harvest cannot wait. It is the shortest period of time in the reproductive growth of your seed. You can leave your seed in your barn and it will still bring forth a harvest when you plant it.

Just like the Lord prepared a harvest for the Israelites, He has prepared a harvest for you. It's *already there*. You just need to go get it.

We are in the season of harvest. If you have to run the combines all night when the grain fields turn golden brown, you do it because you can't wait to bring in the harvest.

We, the church, have crops that have rotted in the field. We have blamed God for not answering our prayer—when in reality, He gave seed to the sower, the sower sowed the seed, and God gave the increase.

The seed will do what it's supposed to do. It is the nature of a seed to reproduce. It is not our responsibility to know how the seed grows. The seed and the soil will do what they are supposed to do.

God will do His part, because He is the one who gives the increase. You have yet to pray a prayer that He did not answer. Every seed you have ever sown has produced a harvest. But because we have not actively known how to harvest our seed, it rotted in the field.

The Lord heard your prayer and He answered that prayer. He multiplied your seed sown.

TIME IS SHRINKING

Genesis 8:22 says, *"While the earth remaineth, seedtime and harvest, and cold and heat, and summer and winter, and day and night shall not cease."*

We can bear witness that, according to Jehovah's covenant, seedtime and harvest, cold and heat, summer and winter, and day and night have not ceased. The world is hinged with evidence to God's never-ending faithfulness.

But if you read carefully, you'll notice that God made no mention of what goes on *between* seedtime and harvest. The closer we get to the soon and imminent return of Jesus Christ, the shorter time will become.

I have a good friend who is a farmer. During harvest time, he will have his combines out all night, if necessary, to bring in the harvest. Why? Because harvest is the shortest time in the planting process. There's a very small window of opportunity to reap the harvest. One year, my friend couldn't get the harvest in fast enough, and a portion of it rotted in the field.

My friends, time is shrinking. There is not going to be any in-between time. The treader of grapes is crushing the grapes under his feet and he hasn't sown any seed yet. As quickly as the seed hits the ground, you are going to harvest it. There are a lot of things still left to do, and that is why God said he would do a quick work in these last days. Your harvest is already there!

UNCLAIMED RICHES FOR THE LAST DAYS

Let me leave you with this final word: it was spring when the children of Israel prepared to pass over the Jordan River. It was during the time of barley harvest, when Jordan overflows all its banks and the river became a torrential current.

The Bible explains it this way,

And as they that bare the ark were come unto Jordan, and the feet of the

> *priests that bare the ark were dipped in the*
> *brim of the water, (for Jordan overfloweth*
> *all his banks all the time of harvest).*
> —*Joshua 3:15*

Why did the Lord bring His people to the Jordan when the snow was melting and the banks of the river were overflowing? Because that's when the harvest was ripening throughout Canaan.

What if there were no crops in the fields ready to harvest? How would the children of Israel be fed when they were across the river and the manna ceased? Their food stood in the fields ready to be gathered. The livelihood of Israelites' enemies was about to become their supply in their newly acquired land! There was a great transfer to God's chosen people!

In this final hour of human history, there's about to be a tremendous transfer of wealth to this generation. The Bible says,

> *For God giveth to a man that is good*
> *in his sight wisdom, and knowledge, and*
> *joy: but to the sinner he giveth travail, to*

gather and to heap up, that he may give to him that is good before God. This also is vanity and vexation of spirit.

—Ecclesiastes 2:26

The apostle James wrote,

Go to now, ye rich men, weep and howl for your miseries that shall come upon you. Your riches are corrupted, and your garments are moth-eaten. Your gold and silver is cankered; and the rust of them shall be a witness against you, and shall eat your flesh as it were fire. Ye have heaped treasure together for the last days. Behold, the hire of the labourers who have reaped down your fields, which is of you kept back by fraud, crieth: and the cries of them which have reaped are entered into the ears of the Lord of sabaoth. Ye have lived in pleasure on the earth, and been wanton; ye have nourished your hearts, as in a day of slaughter. Ye have condemned and killed the just; and he doth not resist you. Be patient therefore, brethren, unto the coming of the Lord. Behold, the husbandman waiteth for the precious fruit of the earth, and hath long patience for it, until he receive the early and latter rain.

—*James 5:1-7*

As I shared with you about Cyrus, the Lord has strategically positioned those whom He will cause to gather large sums of wealth. Why? For the purpose of transferring it to His kingdom for the financing of the Gospel. That's why He says through James, *"Be patient."*

I like to say it this way: *Hold on.* Your harvest is already on the way. Your boss may not be saved, but hold on! The wealth of the wicked is laid up for the just. You may be living paycheck to paycheck, but hold on! God is about to open the windows of heaven and pour you out a blessing you won't be able to contain.

Your harvest begins by placing a demand upon your faith. Maybe you're facing one of the greatest financial burdens of your life. John 16:33 says,

These things I have spoken unto you, that in me ye might have peace. In the world ye shall have tribulation: but be of good cheer; I have overcome the world.

Before you get your seed out of your hand, your promised harvest of unclaimed riches is *already there*, waiting for you. It's time to receive what He has already provided for you!

IT'S ALREADY THERE

Appendix

PROMISES FROM THE WORD

And it shall be, when the Lord thy God shall have brought thee into the land which he sware unto thy fathers, to Abraham, to Isaac, and to Jacob, to give thee great and goodly cities, which thou buildedst not, And houses full of all good things, which thou filledst not, and wells digged, which thou diggedst not, vineyards and olive trees, which thou plantedst not; when thou shalt have eaten and be full; Then beware lest thou forget the Lord, which brought thee forth out of the land of Egypt, from the house of bondage.

—Deuteronomy 6:10-12

But thou shalt remember the Lord thy God: for it is he that giveth thee power to get wealth, that he may establish his covenant which he sware unto thy fathers, as it is this day.

—Deuteronomy 8:18

Then Joshua commanded the officers of the people, saying, Pass through the host, and command the people, saying, Prepare you victuals; for within three days ye shall pass over this Jordan, to go in to possess the land, which the Lord your God giveth you to possess it.

—Joshua 1:10,11

And I have given you a land for which ye did not labour, and cities which ye built not, and ye dwell in them; of the vineyards and oliveyards which ye planted not do ye eat.

—Joshua 24:13

Praise ye the Lord. Blessed is the man that feareth the Lord, that delighteth greatly in his commandments. His seed shall be mighty upon earth: the generation of the upright shall be blessed. Wealth and riches shall be in his house: and his righteousness endureth for ever.

—Psalm 112:1-3

A good man leaveth an inheritance to his children's children: and the wealth of the sinner is laid up for the just.

—Proverbs 13:22

Be not desirous of his dainties: for they are deceitful meat. Labour not to be rich: cease from thine own wisdom.

—Proverbs 23:3,4

For God giveth to a man that is good in his sight wisdom, and knowledge, and joy: but to the sinner he giveth travail, to gather and to heap up, that he may give to him that is good before God. This also is vanity and vexation of spirit.

—Ecclesiastes 2:26

Behold, I will do a new thing; now it shall spring forth; shall ye not know it? I will even make a way in the wilderness, and rivers in the desert.

—Isaiah 43:19

I will go before thee, and make the crooked places straight: I will break in pieces the gates of brass, and cut in sunder the bars of iron: And I will give thee the treasures of darkness, and hidden riches of secret places, that thou mayest know that I, the Lord, which call thee by thy name, am the God of Israel.

—Isaiah 45:2,3

I will also save you from all your uncleannesses: and I will call for the corn, and will increase it, and lay no famine upon you. And I will multiply the fruit of the tree, and the increase of the field, that ye shall receive no more reproach of famine among the heathen.

—Ezekiel 36:29,30

For I know the thoughts that I think toward you, saith the Lord, thoughts of peace, and not of evil, to give you an expected end.

—Jeremiah 29:11

Come, and let us return unto the Lord: for he hath torn, and he will heal us; he hath smitten, and he will bind us up. After two days will he revive us: in the third day he will raise us up, and we shall live in his sight. Then shall we know, if we follow on to know the Lord: his going forth is prepared as the morning; and he shall come unto us as the rain, as the latter and former rain unto the earth.

—Hosea 6:1-3

Behold, the days come, saith the Lord, that the plowman shall overtake the reaper, and the treader of grapes him that soweth seed; and the mountains shall drop sweet wine, and all the hills shall melt.

—Amos 9:13

And he said, So is the kingdom of God, as if a man should cast seed into the ground; And should sleep, and rise night and day, and the seed should spring and grow up, he knoweth not how. For the earth bringeth forth fruit of herself; first the blade, then the ear, after that the full corn in the ear. But when the fruit is brought forth, immediately he putteth in the sickle, because the harvest is come.

—Mark 4:26-29

That the God of our Lord Jesus Christ, the Father of glory, may give unto you the spirit of wisdom and revelation in the knowledge of him: The eyes of your under-standing being enlightened; that ye may know what is the hope of his calling, and what the riches of the glory of his inheri-tance in the saints, And what is the exceed-ing greatness of his power to usward who believe, according to the working of his mighty power.

—Ephesians 1:17-19

But my God shall supply all your need according to his riches in glory by Christ Jesus.

—Philippians 4:19

Giving thanks unto the Father, which hath made us meet to be partakers of the inheritance of the saints in light: Who hath delivered us from the power of darkness, and hath translated us into the kingdom of his dear Son.

—Colossians 1:12,13

But without faith it is impossible to please him: for he that cometh to God must believe that he is, and that he is a rewarder of them that diligently seek him.

—Hebrews 11:6

Beloved, I wish above all things that thou mayest prosper and be in health, even as thy soul prospereth.

—3 John 2

IT'S ALREADY THERE

ABOUT THE AUTHOR

ROD PARSLEY, bestselling author of more than sixty books, is the dynamic pastor of World Harvest Church in Columbus, Ohio, a church with worldwide ministries and a global outreach. As a highly sought-after crusade and conference speaker whom God has raised up as a prophetic voice to America and the world, Parsley is calling people to Jesus Christ through the good news of the Gospel.

He oversees Bridge of Hope Missions, Harvest Preparatory School, World Harvest Bible College, and the *Breakthrough* broadcast, a Christian television and radio show seen by millions and broadcast to nearly 200 countries around the world, including a potential viewing audience of 97% of the homes in the United States and 78% in Canada. *Breakthrough* is carried on 1,400 stations and cable affiliates, including the Trinity Broadcasting Network, the Canadian Vision Network, Armed Forces Radio and Television Network, and in several countries spanning the globe.

Parsley's refreshingly direct style encourages Christians to examine and eradicate sin from their lives. A fearless champion of living God's way, Parsley follows the high standard set by Jesus Christ and compels his readers to do the same. He and his wife Joni have two children, Ashton and Austin.

OTHER BOOKS BY ROD PARSLEY

Ancient Wells, Living Water

At the Cross, Where Healing Begins

Could It Be?

Daily Breakthroughs

The Day Before Eternity

He Came First

No Dry Season (Bestseller)

No More Crumbs (Bestseller)

On the Brink (#1 Bestseller)

Repairers of the Breach

For more information about *Breakthrough*,
World Harvest Church, World Harvest Bible College,
Harvest Preparatory School, or to receive a product list
of the many books, CD's and DVD's
by Rod Parsley, write or call:

Breakthrough/World Harvest Church
P.O. Box 32932
Columbus, OH 43232-0932 USA
(614) 837-1990 (Office)
www.breakthrough.net

World Harvest Bible College
P.O. Box 32901
Columbus, OH 43232-0901 USA
(614) 837-4088
www.worldharvestbiblecollege.org

Harvest Preparatory School
P.O. Box 32903
Columbus, OH 43232-0903 USA
(614) 837-1990
www.harvestprep.org

The Center For Moral Clarity
P.O. Box 32903
Columbus, OH 43232-9926 USA
(613) 382-1188
www.CenterForMoralClarity.net

If you need prayer, Breakthrough Prayer Warriors are
ready to pray with you 24 hours a day, 7 days a week
at: (614) 837-3232